ALLOSAURUS
and Other Dinosaurs of the Rockies

by Dougal Dixon

illustrated by
Steve Weston and **James Field**

PICTURE WINDOW BOOKS
Minneapolis, Minnesota

Picture Window Books
5115 Excelsior Boulevard
Suite 232
Minneapolis, MN 55416
877-845-8392
www.picturewindowbooks.com

Printed in the United States of America.

Library of Congress Cataloging-in-Publication Data
Dixon, Dougal.
Allosaurus and other dinosaurs of the Rockies /
by Dougal Dixon ; illustrated by Steve Weston &
James Field.
p. cm. — (Dinosaur find)
Includes bibliographical references and index.
ISBN-13: 978-1-4048-2748-6 (hardcover)
ISBN-10: 1-4048-2748-X (hardcover)
1. Allosaurus—Juvenile literature. 2. Dinosaurs—Rocky
Mountains Region—Juvenile literature. I. Weston,
Steve, ill. II. Field, James, 1959– ill. III. Title. IV. Series.
QE862.S3D59 2007
567.90978—dc22   2006012131

Acknowledgments
This book was produced for Picture Window Books by
Bender Richardson White, U.K.

Illustrations by James Field (pages 4–5, 7, 11,
15, 19) and Steve Weston (cover and pages 9,
13, 17, 21). Diagrams by Stefan Chabluk.

Photographs: Eyewire Inc. pages 14, 18, 20;
iStockphoto pages 6 (Michelle Radin), 8 (Michael
and Michelle West), 10 (Steffen Foerster), 12 (Linda
McPherson), 16 (Roger Sinasohn).

Consultant: John Stidworthy, Scientific Fellow of
the Zoological Society, London, and former
Lecturer in the Education Department, Natural
History Museum, London.

Reading Adviser: Susan Kesselring, M.A., Literacy
Educator, Rosemount–Apple Valley–Eagan
(Minnesota) School District

Types of dinosaurs

In this book, a red shape at the top of a left-hand page shows the animal was a meat-eater. A green shape shows it was a plant-eater.

Just how big—or small— were they?

Dinosaurs were many different sizes. We have compared their sizes to one of the following:

Chicken
2 feet (60 centimeters) tall
6 pounds (2.7 kilograms)

Adult person
6 feet (1.8 meters) tall
170 pounds (76.5 kg)

Elephant
10 feet (3 m) tall
12,000 pounds
(5,400 kg)

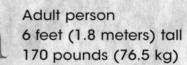

TABLE OF CONTENTS

WHAT'S INSIDE?

Dinosaurs! These dinosaurs lived where the Rocky Mountains are now in North America. Find out how they survived millions of years ago and what they have in common with today's animals.

LIFE IN THE ROCKIES

Dinosaurs lived between 230 million and 65 million years ago. The world did not look the same then. In most parts of the world, the land and seas were not in the same places as today. In dinosaur times, the Rocky Mountains were just beginning to form. At their base were wide plains on which the dinosaurs lived.

The fossils of the dinosaurs shown here—including *Apatosaurus, Ceratosaurus,* and *Ornitholestes*—are now found in the rocks of the Rocky Mountains.

5

APATOSAURUS

Pronunciation:
a-PAT-o-SAW-rus

Apatosaurus and other big, long-necked plant-eaters lived by riverbanks. They migrated in herds from one area of riverside trees to another, feeding on the leaves at the tops of the trees.

Herd animals today

Elk migrate in herds from feeding ground to feeding ground, just like *Apatosaurus* did.

Size Comparison

In dinosaur times, there were wet seasons and dry seasons. *Apatosaurus* herds were always on the move, searching for areas of new plant growth.

Diplodocus had teeth arranged like combs. It used them to scrape leaves and twigs off tree branches. It swallowed stones to help grind up the food. In dry weather, *Diplodocus* would gather around water holes with many other types of dinosaurs.

Thirsty animals today

White-tailed deer gather at water holes to feed and drink, just like *Diplodocus* did long ago.

Size Comparison

Diplodocus needed lots of food and water to keep its huge body active and healthy.

STEGOSAURUS

Pronunciation:
STEG-o-SAW-rus

Stegosaurus had a small, narrow, bird-like head. It also had plates down its back and spikes on its tail. The brightly colored plates were used for signaling. They helped each *Stegosaurus* recognize others of its kind.

Show-offs today

Today, birds use their beaks or feathers to signal to one another, the same way that *Stegosaurus* used its plates.

Size Comparison

Scientists once thought that the large plates on *Stegosaurus* helped the dinosaur stay cool. Studies now show that's not true.

Pronunciation:
AL-o-SAW-rus

Allosaurus was the biggest meat-eater of the Rockies about halfway through the Age of Dinosaurs. As well as hunting and killing live dinosaurs, *Allosaurus* ate those animals that were already dead.

Scavenging today

The turkey vulture eats dead things, just like *Allosaurus* did. It uses its sense of smell to find food.

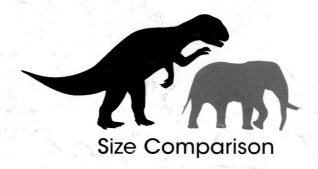

Size Comparison

Allosaurus was one of the fiercest meat-eaters in the North American Rockies.

CERATOSAURUS

Pronunciation:
si-RAT-uh-SAW-rus

Ceratosaurus was an active hunter. It stalked the riverside forests in packs, hunting the big plant-eaters. It had a horn on its nose. Male *Ceratosaurus* may have used the horn as a weapon in fights over females.

Pack hunters today

Packs of wolves prowl through forests, hunting big animals, just as packs of *Ceratosaurus* did.

Size Comparison

Ceratosaurus had
bony structures down
its back. These were
probably for defense.

CAMPTOSAURUS

Pronunciation:
KAMP-tuh-SAW-rus

Camptosaurus was one of the medium-sized plant-eaters from the middle of the Age of Dinosaurs. It lived in the forests that grew along the riverbanks. It could move around on all fours or, when a meat-eater chased it, run away on its hind legs.

Living fossil

The opossum looks like the small mammals that lived alongside *Camptosaurus* in the forests long ago.

Size Comparison

Camptosaurus fed on ferns that grew on the plains where the Rockies now stand.

ORNITHOLESTES

Pronunciation:
or-NITH-o-LESS-teez

Ornitholestes was one of the smaller meat-eating dinosaurs of the time. It hunted small animals on the ground. It may have also chased after pterosaurs and birds as they tried to fly away.

Busy eaters today

The raccoon feeds on a variety of things on the ground or in the trees. It eats all kinds of meat, like *Ornitholestes* did.

Size Comparison

Ornitholestes hunted for little animals, both in the damp forests and on the dry plains.

Pronunciation:
KAM-uh-ruh-SAW-rus

Camarasaurus was one of the long-necked plant-eaters. It had big nostrils and a wide mouth. Like the other long-necks, *Camarasaurus* moved in large herds from one feeding ground to another.

Migrating today

Snow geese and blue geese travel far to find sources of plant food, like *Camarasaurus* did long ago.

Size Comparison

With its long neck, *Camarasaurus* could eat from the ground, from bushes, and from the tops of high trees.

WHERE DID THEY GO?

Dinosaurs are extinct, which means that none of them are alive today. Scientists study rocks and fossils to find clues about what happened to dinosaurs.

People have different explanations about what happened. Some people think a huge asteroid hit Earth and caused all sorts of climate changes, which caused the dinosaurs to die. Others think volcanic eruptions caused the climate to change and that killed the dinosaurs. No one knows for sure what happened to all of the dinosaurs.

Glossary

ferns—plants with finely divided leaves known as fronds; ferns are common in damp woods and along rivers

fossils—the remains of a plant or animal that lived between thousands and millions of years ago

herds—large groups of animals that move, feed, and sleep together

horns—pointed structures on the head, made of a hard, shiny substance

mammals—warm-blooded animals that have hair and drink mother's milk when they are young

migrate—to regularly move from place to place to find food, shelter, or a mate

packs—groups of animals that hunt and kill together

plains—large areas of flat land with few large plants

pterosaurs—flying animals related to dinosaurs

signaling—making a sign, warning, or hint

To Learn More

At the Library

Clark, Neil, and William Lindsay. *1001 Facts About Dinosaurs.* New York: Backpack Books, Dorling Kindersley, 2002.

Gray, Susan H. *Allosaurus.* Chanhassen, Minn.: Child's World, 2004.

Sabuda, Robert, and Matthew Reinhart. *Dinosaurs.* Cambridge, Mass.: Candlewick Press, 2005.

On the Web

FactHound offers a safe, fun way to find Internet sites related to this book. All of the sites on FactHound have been researched by our staff.

1. Visit *www.facthound.com*
2. Type in this special code for age-appropriate sites: 140482748X
3. Click on the FETCH IT button.

Your trusty FactHound will fetch the best sites for you!

Index

Look for all of the books in the Dinosaur Find series: